The Wogglebug's Methods to Finding Lost Things

Copyright © 2014 by Cynthia Hanson

Printed in the U.S.A.
Exclusively for WogglebugLove Productions.

First Edition: October 2014

ISBN: #978-0692227084
(WogglebugLove Productions)

The Wogglebug's Methods to Finding Lost Things

by Cynthia Hanson

This is exclusively for

WogglebugLove Productions

Hello to all my friends again! I would like to take the opportunity this time to relate to you a story about how one day I gained a new lesson about how to find things I misplace. Then ended up being able to teach others the same, only to gain another lesson for myself! It all began one morning that started out just like most others do for me. I woke up and felt happy as I greeted the sun shining from behind my window as I got out on the right side of my bed.

Then I got myself dressed neatly. I put into my pockets my accessories I always carry with me. These include my gold watch, my notebook, my pencil case, my calling cards. All of these I found easily and put them in place. But then I suddenly didn't know where my handkerchief was. This puzzled and also worried me! For my handkerchief is important for me to have with me. I started to worry of what if I couldn't find it.

But I reminded myself not to worry, and reassured myself I would find my handkerchief by logically retracing my steps from the events of yesterday before I went to bed. Being thoroughly educated I understand how it is a good idea to start back to the last place you were if you've lost something. I left my bedroom and went into the foyer.

I remembered the night before I had stayed up until about midnight while playing chess with the Frogman.

After I found no recollection of leaving my handkerchief in the foyer, I retraced my steps from yesterday into the Royal Library.

I remembered I'd spent a few hours there doing some detailed research into things I was interested in. I remembered I'd sat beside the window where there was the most light source. So I approached this area.

I searched around, trying to recollect where I may have left my handkerchief last. I was startled when I suddenly felt a slight tingle in the tip of my nose. This quite alarmed me as I pressed my forefinger firmly under my nose. I mustn't sneeze until I've found my handkerchief. Much to my relief the feeling in my nose left after a moment. Then I left the library, knowing there must have been a bit of dust in it.

My urgency to find my handkerchief had elevated considerably. I quickly went to the very next place I remembered I was at during yesterday, the Royal Gardens. I and the Frogman along with our friend Sylvie had a picnic there in the afternoon.

Sylvie had taught us how to play tennis and hopscotch with her. Then we'd had a contest about which of us could name the most insects likely to come to which plants there were around us. The Frogman naming a few I wasn't sure I knew of had been my reason for studying in the library afterward.

While I looked around the areas, I was suddenly startled once again when the feel of an oncoming sneeze entered my nose again. I quickly pressed my finger under my nose again and turned away from an area of flowers near me. I ought to have known at this time of year the pollen levels are high. Not that I am allergic, but I just have a sensitive feeler to my nose.

I left the gardens and hurried back indoors. Once inside the need to sneeze left me once again. But I was aware I might not be so lucky next time. I felt quite distressed by now. I had to think very hard about where I must have last had my handkerchief with me. My thoughts took over and I quickly darted into the next corridor. I had an inkling in me I would get lucky if I kept moving forward in the direction.

Suddenly I was met by my friend Sylvie in the corridor. She noticed I was distressed. "Mr. Wogglebug, what is wrong?" she asked. I replied, "I can't remember where I left my handkerchief, and I..I..ahh..." I felt the need to sneeze come to me again and pressed my forefinger under my nose to halt it. "I am in a predicament because of it!" Sylvie saw this easily. She seemed to think quickly.

Then a memory flashed unto her. She explained to me the very next thing I needed to remember. "It must still be in the pocket of the vest you had on yesterday," she exclaimed. "Which you put into the laundry basket after a bit of pineapple juice was spilled onto it during our picnic when one of those snap-dragonflies flew near and startled us."

I instantly knew she was right, and this was the next thing for me to remember! We hurried down the hall, turned a corner and then found where the clean laundry baskets were. I started to reach into them, but started to feel the urge to sneeze again and instead pressed my forefinger under my nose. Sylvie reached into the basket's bundle and quickly found my handkerchief and kindly handed it to me as I took it most gratefully.

I at once covered my nose and mouth very firmly with my clean handkerchief, turned myself around and let my sneeze out fully into it. "Ahh.. ahhh... AHH... CHOO-OOO!" A bit heavily from being held in for a while, but at least no germs were spread whatsoever. "Oh my! Gesundheit, my friend!" Sylvie exclaimed afterward.

I felt so much better, not to mentioned relieved now. "Thank you, my dear," I said as I turned around again. "Especially for being there for me at the right moment!" I hugged Sylvie close to me for a moment to emphasize this. "You are a very clever, quick-witted girl, you know!"

Later I related these events to the Frogman as we had our evening fireside chat. "Then I of course had to wash my handkerchief again!" I concluded with a laugh. "The point is I've learned how it is wise to retrace one's steps when needing to find a personally lost item, in addition to getting a bit of help if need be." "Very true," said the Frogman. "In times of urgency the mind takes over to outsmart any odds, as you and Sylvie proved."

I knew he was right. I also knew I'm not the only one capable of losing personal items. I decided to devise a way to help others be able to find missing items in just as effective and even better a way than I followed. For the next six months, I secretly created a new invention meant to do so. I named my invention a theory-detector. A device which responds to my voice commands, and a digital language I invented for it.

One day Professor Knowitall came to me and reported he had lost his silver pocket watch, a rich woman had lost her hand mirror, and a sheriff had lost his badge, and a coach had lost his whistle. I put my new device to use. I spoke of the objects lost into the voice box, typed in codes about the circumstances surrounding them I heard. Then the theory-detector gave me the best possible theories of them. It said they were all together in one remote location. Which was the gazebo in the backyard behind the palace! So I rushed off to this location with everyone following behind me.

Once we were in the Enchanted Forest, we found a large white and yellow cockatoo bird. It seemed because cockatoos are attracted to shiny and silver objects it had snatched all of these items from these people when they weren't looking. But now thanks to me and my invention they all got them back. I took my invention on a bigger adventure one day but that is another story.

To Learn More About the Wogglebug Franchise Visit

https://www.WogglebugloveProductions.com